Good Glide

The science of ski waxing

U.S. Ski Team

Sports Medicine Series

Good Glide

The science of ski waxing

Leif Torgersen

Ski Research Scientist
Swix Wax Company
Oslo, Norway

Translated by Michael Brady

Published under the auspices
of the United States Ski Team by
Human Kinetics Publishers, Inc.
Champaign, Illinois

Library of Congress Cataloging-in-Publication Data

Torgersen, Leif.
  Good glide.

  Translation of: God glid.
  1. Ski waxing. I. Title.
GV855.5.W39T6713   1985   796.93   85-14410
ISBN: 0-87322-033-1

Production Director: Sara Chilton
Editor: Peg Goyette
Typesetter: Yvonne Sergent
Text and Cover Design: Julie Szamocki
Text Layout: Janet Davenport
Photographs: Michael Brady
  Central Institute for Industrial Research (pp. 36, 42, 77)
  Lori Adamski, U.S. Ski Team (pp. vii, 52, 70)
Drawings: U.S. Dept. of Agriculture
  Gro Roenneberg (p. 31)

ISBN: 0-87322-033-1   *TOC*
Copyright © by H. Aschehoug & Co. (W. Nygaard) A/S, Oslo, 1983

Printed in the United States of America

10 9 8 7 6 5 4 3 2 1

Human Kinetics Publishers, Inc.
Box 5076, Champaign, IL 61820

Contents

Preface

The title and subtitle of this book reflect the character of modern waxing for ski racing. As always, the aim is speed, but waxing for speed is more than just applying wax to skis. It also involves many other factors, such as the properties of ski bases.

The best way to view the entire art of waxing is to consider the ski base and ski wax together, as a single unit inter-acting with snow. Each waxing job then amounts to "designing" a base-and-wax unit that interacts as well as possible with snow. This means that a knowledge of the complexities of snow and the processes governing its changes is necessary for successful waxing. A major part of this book, then, is devoted to snow because the best waxers are those who best judge snow.

Waxing involves practical skills, not only in the preparation of ski bases and the application of waxes but also in the judging of snow and the various meteorological factors influencing waxing. When a person is faced with a waxing problem, no verbal explanation can replace a clear picture of what actually goes on when waxed skis make contact with snow. Therefore, this book contains many illustrations so the reader can see what is being explained.

This book is primarily for cross-country skiers, for waxing is more crucial in cross-country than in any other skiing discipline. Yet the basics of glide waxing for cross-country and Alpine skiing as well as for ski jumping are the same. Cross-country skiers need grip waxes for kick, and Alpine skiers must file their edges, but both need the same fundamental knowledge of snow in order to wax well. So this book is written for all ski racers as well as for skilled recreational skiers who wish to know more about their sport.

This English language edition is revised and updated from the original Norwegian edition of August 1983. The products described and illustrated in this book are 1985 products.

Oslo, May 1, 1985
Leif Torgersen

1 Snow Makes Skiing Possible

Individual views about snow are divided. People who live in "snow country" associate snow with winter and cold. Some of them think of snow only in terms of slippery streets and roads, snow plowing, and traffic delays, all of which they could well do without. In contrast, millions of people in other parts of the world never have seen snow and never will. But avid skiers love snow and look forward to it every winter. As skiers, they should know something about this basic element of their sport. They should have a knowledge of snow and how it is affected and changed by meteorological conditions, which in turn will give them a better understanding of waxing.

Snow in the atmosphere

Skiers are mostly interested in snow on the ground. But to understand snow we must start at the beginning, when snow is still in the atmosphere. This is where snow crystals are formed and precipitation starts. Varying atmospheric conditions create the infinite variety of snow crystals that later combine to form snow cover on the ground. Precipitation in the form of snow may occur whenever the temperature is low enough. In addition, there must be a surplus of atmospheric moisture and the conditions must be right for that moisture to become precipitation.

A newly formed ice crystal, or *embryo crystal*, is very small, usually no larger than 75 μm (1 μm is 1/1000 of a millimeter, about 4/10,000 of an inch). It falls slowly (at about 1 ft/min) and has a simple form, usually a hexagonal (six-sided) wafer, or *plate*. Ice crystals grow further by sublimation (direct depositing of water vapor in solid form) to become the beautiful snow crystals you can study with the naked eye. Individual crystals sometimes stick together, typically in heavy snowfalls when the temperature is near freezing (0° C, 32° F), to form larger snowflakes.

Snow crystals often fall through layers of air containing

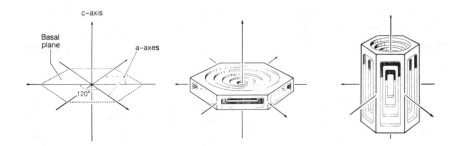

The simplest atmospheric ice crystals are hexagonal plates or columns. Temperature primarily determines along which crystallographic axis a crystal will form.

supercooled water droplets, which freeze on the crystals as *rime*. By the time these crystals reach the ground, their original shape may be obliterated. Snow deposited on the ground can then be rime-coated to varying degrees, taking the form of symmetrical crystals or crystal fragments.

Snow crystals develop differently, depending on the temperature and moisture in the air layers where they are formed and on the conditions in the air layers through which they pass in falling to the ground. The various types of crystal have

been classified (Magono & Lee, 1966) as shown in the schematic charts on pages 5 and 6. The most common types are:

- plates,
- stellar crystals,
- columns,
- needles,
- stellar forms in three dimensions,
- capped columns with plates on ends or sides,
- irregular forms (not classified).

The meteorological conditions that favor formation of various types of crystal are beyond the scope of this book. If you are interested in them, there are many meteorological textbooks on the subject. For the purpose of this book—waxing and skiing—you need be concerned only with a few crystal forms.

Waxing may seem difficult whenever snow crystals are coated with rime or frozen water vapor. Even at temperatures that would normally call for hard waxes (such as Blue), cross-country skiers find that softer waxes (Blue Extra or Violet) are needed for grip on this type of snow. At the opposite extreme are conditions in which a light dusting of snow falls from a relatively thin cloud layer, often with the sun shining through. The crystals usually are separate and are characterized by hard edges that can dig deeply into wax. If the air temperature is just between the range of two waxes (such as between Green and Blue), then it's best to select the harder wax.

Low-pressure fronts usually bring precipitation, but the rate of precipitation may vary. Typical for winter snowfalls in the snow belt are average accumulations of snow at a rate of 4/10 of an inch per hour, equivalent to a liquid precipitation rate of 4/100 of an inch per hour.

Snow density can vary considerably. For new snow, typical densities range from 4.4 to 7.5 pounds per cubic foot. Wind can pack new snow to greater densities, up to 16 pounds per cubic foot, whereas older, compacted snow cover can range up to 32 to 38 pounds per cubic foot.

Snow on the ground

Snow on the ground is described and classified a bit dif-

	N1a Elementary needle		**C1f** Hollow column		**P2b** Stellar crystal with sectorlike ends
	N1b Bundle of elementary needles		**C1g** Solid thick plate		**P2c** Dendritic crystal with plates at ends
	N1c Elementary sheath		**C1h** Thick plate of skeleton form		**P2d** Dendritic crystal with sectorlike ends
	N1d Bundle of elementary sheaths		**C1i** Scroll		**P2e** Plate with simple extensions
	N1e Long solid column		**C2a** Combination of bullets		**P2f** Plate with sector-like extensions
	N2a Combination of needles		**C2b** Combination of columns		**P2g** Plate with den-dritic extensions
	N2b Combination of sheaths		**P1a** Hexagonal plate		**P3a** Two-branched crystal
	N2c Combination of long solid columns		**P1b** Crystal with sec-torlike branches		**P3b** Three-branched crystal
	C1a Pyramid		**P1c** Crystal with broad branches		**P3c** Four-branched crystal
	C1b Cup		**P1d** Stellar crystal		**P4a** Broad branch crystal with 12 branches
	C1c Solid bullet		**P1e** Ordinary dendritic crystal		**P4b** Dendritic crystal with 12 branches
	C1d Hollow bullet		**P1f** Fernlike crystal		**P5** Malformed crystal
	C1e Solid column		**P2a** Stellar crystal with plates at ends		**P6a** Plate with special plates

	P6b Plate with spatial dendrites		**CP3d** Plate with scrolls at ends		**R3c** Graupel-like snow with nonrimed extensions
	P6c Stellar crystal with spatial plates		**S1** Side planes		**R4a** Hexagonal graupel
	P6d Stellar crystal with spatial dendrites		**S2** Scalelike side planes		**R4b** Lump graupel
	P7a Radiating assemblage of plates		**S3** Combination of side planes, bullets and columns		**R4c** Conelike graupel
	P7b Radiating assemblage of dendrites		**R1a** Rimed needle crystal		**I1** Ice particle
	CP1a Column with plates		**R1b** Rimed columnar crystal		**I2** Rimed particle
	CP1b Column with dendrites		**R1c** Rimed plate or sector		**I3a** Broken branch
	CP1c Multiple capped column		**R1d** Rimed stellar crystals		**I3b** Rimed broken branch
	CP2a Bullet with plates		**R2a** Densely rimed plate or sector		**I4** Miscellaneous
	CP2b Bullet with dendrites		**R2b** Densely rimed stellar crystal		**G1** Minute column
					G2 Germ of skeleton form
	CP3a Stellar crystal with needles		**R2c** Stellar crystal with rimed spatial branches		**G3** Minute hexagonal plate
	CP3b Stellar crystal with columns		**R3a** Graupel-like snow of hexagonal type		**G4** Minute stellar crystal
					G5 Min. assem. of plates
	CP3c Stellar crystal with scrolls at ends		**R3b** Graupel-like snow of lump type		**G6** Irregular germ

ferently than snow in the atmosphere. In one respect it is simpler: There are fewer crystal types. However, new problems arise because snow on the ground undergoes continual change and different types of snow are associated with those changes.

Snow crystals are among the most unstable structures in nature; their metamorphism begins as soon as they are deposited on the ground. And, because there are periods of dryness as well as precipitation during the winter, different layers of snow cover vary in thickness, hardness, and structure. The characteristics of new layers depend on the snow crystal structure during a snowfall and on the prevailing meteorological conditions thereafter.

A layer of snow can generally be regarded as a porous material. The snow surface and the underlying layers consist of solid water, or ice, in a skeleton-like structure. The cavities are filled with air and water vapor which circulate between the ice and snow particles. The size of the cavities, or *pore volume*, indicates the density of the snow or how hard it is packed. Ice crystals and water vapor can exist together when the air is cold and the snow is dry.

The liquid phase, water, may be either "bound" in molecule-thin films of water on ice and snow particles, or "free" to move between ice and snow particles by capillary force or gravity. The presence of "free" water depends on the snow cover, or a part of it, having reached its maximum temperature of 0° C (32° F).

Density is one of the most important and most characteristic properties of snow. But snow can further be classified according to age, moisture content,

Snow classified according to moisture content

Snow type	Properties	Possible cross-country wax for new snow
Dry snow	Temperature usually below 0º C (32º F), but if the air is extremely dry (such as a Chinook wind), snow can be dry up to freezing. Handfull of snow does not pack to a snowball	Green or Blue wax
Slightly moist snow	Snow doesn't seem wet Can be pressed into clumps	Violet wax
Moist snow	0º C (32º F) snow temperature Snow seems wet, but moisture can't be forced out Snow packs well to a snowball	Red wax or Yellow Klisterwax
Wet snow	Water can be pressed out of snow and can be seen between snow crystals, but snow still contains some air	Yellow Klisterwax
Very wet snow	Water runs out (slushy, sloppy) Snow essentially water-soaked; very little air left in pores	Yellow or Red Klisterwax

porosity, snow crystal size, hardness, and shape.

Particle changes in snow cover

Mechanical effects and breakdown

Mechanical effects are most important in new snow layers composed of dry to moist snow crystals. The forces involved include collisions between crystals driven by the wind and compression from the weight of deposited snow. Crystal shape also plays a role: Star-shaped crystals are most subject to mechanical damage.

Wind-driven snow can begin to break down when it is still in the air. It mixes and swirls together with older snow, and the difference between old and new snow is not discernible unless seen through a microscope. Friction and wear against snow surfaces rapidly grind the particles, making them smaller and rounder.

The weight of new snow layers also causes snow to break down, and this effect increases with the thickness of the layers deposited. For instance, in a 20-inch layer of new snow the force of weight on the crystals at the bottom is of course greater than on those near the top. Thus, for the same depth of new snow, wet snow is altered more by its own weight than is dry snow simply because it is heavier. Mechanical compression may increase snow density from approximately 5 to 6 pounds per cubic foot to 12 to 16 pounds per cubic foot.

Formation by breakdown—destructive metamorphism

The process of destructive metamorphism is illustrated in the drawing on page 10. Water vapor pressure is greater at the sharp, pointed parts of a crystal (convex surfaces) than at the rounded parts (concave surfaces). In other words, the vapor saturation varies from the protrusions to the indentations of a snow crystal. Sublimation will

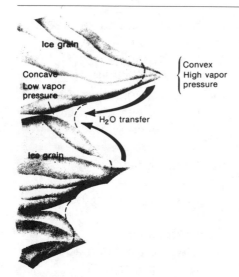

Water molecules tend to transfer from convexities to concavities because vapor pressure is higher over a convex ice surface than over a concave ice surface.

transport water molecules away from protrusions, which round them off.

Water vapor then accumulates and condenses in the indentations; this is why ice or snow

crystals are thermodynamically unstable. Breakdown is the process of establishing balance.

Deep in a layer of snow the process results in larger crystals forming at the expense of smaller crystals, which then slowly disappear. Gradually, most of the particles will be about 2/100 to 4/100 of an inch in diameter. Particles in contact with one another also become interconnected with small ice bridges, or *necks*. These points of contact between crystals are concave indentations, which accumulate condensed vapor.

The process goes on in snow layers when the temperature is below freezing, but in that case temperature differences are small. The snow is said to be *isothermal*, and the metamorphic process is called *isothermal metamorphism*. Differences in crystal surface curvatures are the primary cause of the metamorphism, but temperature determines the speed at which it

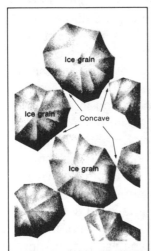 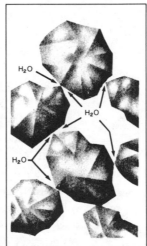 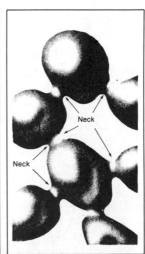

Weight presses snow grains into contact. The joining process forms the ice skeleton.

occurs. It can be very rapid when temperatures are near the melting point at 0º C (32º F). The lower the temperature, the longer the crystals retain their original form. At temperatures near freezing, snow-melt water alters the metamorphic process; this process is shown on page 13.

Formation by constructive metamorphism

Vertical temperature differences in snow cover cause constructive metamorphism. Snow is a good insulator. For instance, when the air temperature is -20⁰ C (-4⁰ F), the temperature 20 inches deep in a snow cover might be around -5⁰ C (23⁰ F). This difference produces a temperature gradient of:

$$g_m = \frac{-20^0\ C - (-5^0\ C)}{50\ cm} = -0.3^0\ \frac{C}{cm} = 1.4^0\ \frac{F}{in.}$$

Water vapor pressure depends on temperature, so such a temperature difference in a snow cover results in water molecules being transported from the warmer to the colder layers. When water molecules move in this manner, they tend to be deposited directly on snow particles and not on the contact points or necks between particles. This means that the crystals tend to grow and the connections between them diminish.

The crystals thus formed are layered and have a cup or scroll shape. They are called *cup crystals*. For skiers, cup crystals in a snow cover spell danger of avalanches. Any sudden settling of snow indicates a failure in the supporting ability of the underlying snow, as caused by temperature-gradient metamorphism.

Constructive and destructive metamorphism often occur together in a layer of snow, but at any given time one of the two usually dominates. In new snow layers the crystals are sharp and destructive metamorphism usually dominates. Later, when the snow particles are rounded, constructive metamorphism occurs. Cup crystals form easily in a light snow cover when there is a large difference in temperature between the surface and the ground.

Snow density increases in late winter. At densities greater than 22 pounds per cubic foot, snow

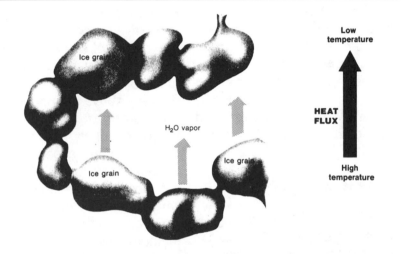

Water vapor flows from regions of higher to regions of lower temperature in the ice skeleton.

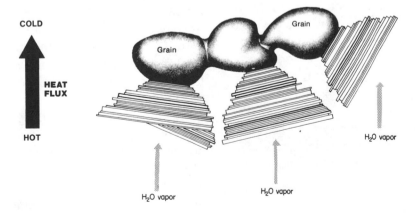

Temperature gradient metamorphism forms cup crystals.

contains little air and may instead contain large amounts of free water. Under these conditions vertical temperature differences are small and water vapor diffusion is correspondingly small. Melt metamorphism and destructive metamorphism then dominate.

Melt metamorphism

Thus far we've been talking about cold snow which contains very little free water. As soon as liquid water is present, however, a new and extremely powerful formation process enters the picture. Free water in a snow layer is common and occurs in late winter, in the spring, or otherwise in periods of mild winter weather. Free water comes from two sources: melted snow, or external sources such as rain.

Rain can increase snow moisture content considerably.

But contrary to popular opinion, rain plays only a minor role in the melting of snow. It takes 80 calories of heat to melt one gram of snow, and rain at a few degrees above freezing just doesn't contain enough thermal energy to supply that level of heat. Changes caused by repeated melting and freezing are most common in late winter, when daytime sunshine melts snow and subfreezing nighttime temperatures refreeze it.

Initial melting causes rapid changes in a snow cover and it begins to sink as many of the pores fill with water. Warming melts the smaller crystals first, then the water from the melting fills the spaces between and affects the surfaces of the larger crystals.

The melting of a snow cover is a complex process. Weather conditions begin the melting. Melt-water flows downward, but it can refreeze at underlying layers. A snow cover can retain large amounts of water if it melts slowly. Only when an entire snow cover is at the same temperature, isothermal at 0⁰ C (32⁰ F), will it melt rapidly. The pores fill with water; the snow cover is said to be *mature*, and run-off starts.

Hoarfrost and ice formation on snow surfaces

Hoarfrost and ice are forms of water in its solid phase. They are not snow, but they frequently occur on snow surfaces. Hoarfrost can be deposited whenever the humidity in the air is close to saturation, making it super-saturated with respect to ice. Vapor can then *sublimate*, or condense directly on ice surfaces, forming hoarfrost.

Hoar crystals usually occur as flakes or plates. Skis gliding on a hoarfrost surface produce a squeaking sound as the crystals break. Glide is good because the friction between the crystals and the gliding skis is lower than with ordinary snow. Hoarfrost is usually deposited by mild winds on cold, clear nights.

Rime is another form of ice deposit. Rime is formed when supercooled drops of atmospheric vapor or fog precipitate on a surface of snow.

A third type of ice deposit is *glaze*, which occurs when super-cooled raindrops or drops of fog precipitate on a snow surface and freeze. Ski tracks will glaze easily in this case, and glide can be excellent.

A combination of weather conditions can produce a fourth type of surface of interest to skiers. Cold air, radiation of heat from a snow surface, and evaporation normally will cool

Meteorological conditions at snow surfaces

The following is an overview of how temperature, radiation, wind, and humidity affect snow and its skiability.

Temperature

Temperature is a vital ingredient for snow skiability and wax choice. Here we differentiate between *snow temperature* and *air temperature*. Customary meteorological practice

snow, while absorbed solar energy warms snow.

Sometimes these conditions can combine to melt snow immediately *under* the surface. The snow-melt water subsequently freezes, forming a thin, crisp film of ice on the surface. The ice acts like glass in a greenhouse. That is, it doesn't melt but the snow underneath it does. As the snow melts, it becomes wet and then it sinks, pulling away from the surface ice to form air bubbles. Skis glide extremely well on such a glasslike surface. Downhill speeds can be high, sometimes too high for safe skiing on the apparent frictionless surface. In some places, particularly downhills with southern exposure, solar heating can be considerable and a skier can risk breaking through the thin film of ice into the underlying slush.

Typical meteorological instrument house used at major international races.

measures air temperature 5 to 6½ feet above the ground, in a ventilated housing that is shielded from the sun. Temperatures as measured by thermometers on house or building walls tend to be inaccurate, especially when the thermometers are exposed to the sun.

Snow temperature should be taken just under the snow surface. But that's not always easy. If the surface is of crust or ice, it is difficult to get a thermometer down into the snow. If the surface is extremely loose, the thermometer may sink too deep and therefore not read surface temperature correctly.

In practice, most recreational skiers simply glance at any thermometer they see. Racers need to be more careful, however, so usually they measure snow temperature as well.

At temperatures below freezing, snow temperature and air temperature are fairly close. But at temperatures above freezing when snow contains free water and snow temperature is 0⁰ C (32⁰ F), snow and air temperatures can differ considerably. In these conditions racers should check air humidity and snow water content.

Heat exchange and radiation conditions

Whenever snow is warmer than the surrounding air, it loses heat to the atmosphere. Conversely, whenever the atmosphere is warmer than the snow, the snow gains heat from the air. This type of heat exchange is slow if there is little air movement. But the more turbulent the air movement above the snow, the more rapid the heat exchange.

Extremely humid air can be saturated with respect to the underlying snow. Moisture in the air can then be deposited on the snow, which speeds the transfer of heat from air to snow. Conversely, heat from the snow is returned to the atmosphere if warm, dry air blows over the snow. Water vapor molecules can sublimate directly from the snow to the air. Air temperature can rise to 7^0-8^0 C (45^0-47^0 F) without much effect on a snow cover, provided the sun is low in the sky. If the snow is new, softer waxes such as Red Special or Red may prove too sticky. If the snow is older, "klister snow," the conditions still call for ice klister, *not* wet-snow klister. A mixture of Blue and Violet klister, maybe with a bit of Silver klister mixed in, might work best.

Falling snow either warms a snow cover or is warmed by it, depending on the relative temperatures involved. Rain can only warm snow but, as previously discussed, the heat that rain supplies is relatively small.

Difficulties in measuring surface snow temperature are discussed on page 16. Surface temperature is also affected considerably by radiation, two components of which are important: *short wave* radiation from the sun, and *long wave* radiation from the earth.

Solar radiation intensity depends on

- geographical position (latitude),
- date,
- time of day,
- cloud cover,
- exposure and slope of terrain.

Part of the short-wave radiation that reaches a snow surface is reflected back to the atmosphere. This property of snow is described by a term borrowed from astronomy: *albedo*, the ratio of light reflected to the light received. If the albedo is 90%, a value typical of fresh snow, then only 10% of the light received is absorbed to heat the snow cover. As snow ages and its water content increases, it absorbs more of the radiation it receives. Spring snow can have an albedo of about 50%.

The earth radiates heat. In the form of long-wave (infrared) radiation, this heat is absorbed by the atmosphere, such as by cloud cover, and is reradiated to the earth and outward to space. Actually, the effects of long-wave radiation cannot be described exactly. They depend on the temperature of the snow surface, the temperature of the cloud cover, and the distributions of humidity and temperature in the atmosphere.

For skiers, the practical results are that on cold, clear nights, snow surfaces remain colder than air temperature because emitted long-wave radiation escapes to space. Sudden overcasts cause snow temperature to rise rapidly because the long-wave radiation to space is less efficient or because the snow absorbs radiation from the warmer clouds. This is why testing wax and skis when the cloud cover changes can produce erratic test results.

The various processes of heat exchange described above can be summarized as follows:

- Snow surface temperature will follow a gradual rise of air temperature up to a maximum of 0° C (32° F). Further heating will not raise the temperature of the snow but will increase its water content.
- Snow surface temperature will follow a gradual fall of air temperature.

- Exceptions to these two trends occur when evening and night skies are clear. Long-wave radiation to space can be so great that snow temperature falls, regardless of air temperature variations.
- Even when the midwinter sun is low in the sky, morning air temperatures can rise while snow surfaces lose heat to space, which causes the snow surface temperature to remain relatively constant. This phenomenon is typical for northern latitudes such as Scandinavia or Alaska, and for terrain on northern ex- posures.

Effects of altitude on temperature

Normally, air temperature decreases about 0.6⁰ C per 100-meter increase in altitude (about 0.3⁰ F per 100-ft altitude). On sunny days the difference can be far greater, particularly at abrupt borders between stands of trees and mountain walls where it may be as much as 1⁰ C per 100 meters altitude (0.55⁰ F per 100 ft), because the albedo of trees is lower than that of rock. This is a useful tip to remember when skiing at higher altitudes.

Temperature inversion is a reversal of the normal temperature decrease with altitude increase and results in warm air on top of cold. On clear, calm nights, cold air sinks to lower altitudes and is trapped there by topographical forma- tions because it is heavier than the warmer air at higher altitudes. Inversion occurs most frequently in midwinter cold spells at high barometric pressures. Often the temperature at the floor of a valley, bowl, or cirque may be 15⁰ C (27⁰ F) lower than the temperature on the surrounding ridges.

Wind

Falling snow driven by strong wind mixes with snow surface particles and packs into drifts. The snow particles grind against each other and against the surface of snow on the ground. They wear down, often to a 10th of their original size. Windpack snow in slabs and cornices can be two to four times as dense as snow that fell with no wind.

The small particles and many contact points between particles in windpack snow cause skis to glide poorly on it. It is a drawback that cannot be overcome by waxing. The best compromise is to wax according to temperature, carefully scraping glide wax and applying grip wax in thinner layers than usual.

Visability is reduced when falling snow is driven by wind. Snow will drift when wind speeds exceed 5 to 7 meters per second (16 to 23 ft/sec). Further increases in wind speed will increase the height of the snowdrift; at speeds of 10 m/sec (32 ft/sec), drifting height is greater than the height of an adult skier and visability is reduced to less than 15 feet.

Air humidity

Air humidity is important in judging snow and selecting wax. Because humidity is neglected in most discussions of waxing and because it usually is poorly described in school texts, it is reviewed briefly here.

The water vapor content of the atmosphere is described in terms of *humidity*. Atmospheric water vapor is *not* like steam escaping from boiling water. The visible steam escaping from a pot of boiling water is made up of many small drops of condensed water. On the other hand, atmospheric water vapor is an invisible gas. But it can condense and become visible, as in dew, fog, and clouds.

Humidity expressed in percent is *relative humidity*. Relative humidity is the ratio between the amount of water vapor in a given volume of air to the maximum amount of water vapor the same volume of air can hold at the same temperature and pressure, expressed as a percentage. For example, at normal sea-level pressure (1013 millibar) and a temperature of 20º C (68º F), a cubic meter (about 10 cubic feet) of air can hold 17.3 grams of water vapor before condensation occurs. If that cubic meter of air contains only 6 grams of water vapor, it holds $6/17.3 \times 100\% = 36.8\%$ as much water vapor as possible. So its relative humidity is 36.8%.

Relative humidity is referred to in weather reports. But *absolute humidity*, the amount of water vapor in the air in grams per cubic meter, is what's important in the various processes involving snow. The amount of water vapor that air can hold depends on pressure and temperature. At normal sea-level pressure (1013 millibar), air at -18º C (0º F) can hold 1.29 g/m³ of water vapor. At air temperatures below freezing, saturation is expressed relative to water (supercooled) and relative to ice. The figure of 1.29 g/m³ applies to contact with water. Relative to an ice surface, the figure is 1.08 g/m³; it increases to 4.85 g/m³ at 0º C, 9.4 g/m³ at 10º C, 17.3 g/m³ at 20º C, and 30.4 g/m³ at 30º C.

Increases of water vapor above that which the atmosphere can hold appear as condensation on surfaces and objects that are at the same temperature or colder than the air. As air containing moisture cools, it reaches a temperature at which it is saturated and condensation occurs. This is the *dew point*, at which moisture condenses out of the air as dew or water droplets.

As temperature falls below the dew point, more water vapor condenses. The amount of vapor in a mass of air can be calculated from its dew point because at that temperature the relative humidity is always 100%.

Humidity is usually measured by a *hygrometer*, which directly indicates relative humidity. Accurate humidity measurements are made using a *psychrometer*, an instrument containing two thermometers, the bulb of one kept moist while the other is dry.

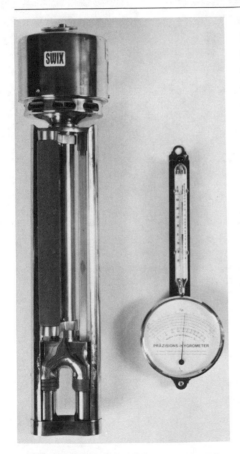

Psychrometer (left) and hygrometer (right).

dicates a lower temperature than the dry thermometer. The dryer the air, the greater the evaporation and the greater the difference in the readings of the two thermometers. If the air is saturated (relative humidity 100%), there will be no evaporation and the readings will be alike. Tables are used to translate thermometer readings to relative humidities. Hygrometers are less accurate than psychrometers, but for practical measurements of humidity they are more convenient to use.

At subfreezing temperature, solid ice water molecules in the snow change directly to water vapor without going through a liquid water stage. For a given temperature, air may be saturated with respect to ice and snow but less than saturated with respect to water.

Evaporation cools the bulb of the wet thermometer, so it in-

2 Friction on Snow and Ice—The Basics of Skiing

Gliding friction

Friction is the resistance to movement that occurs when one object slides over the surface of another. According to classical friction theory, the force necessary to overcome friction and cause motion is directly proportional to an object's weight, independent of the size of the surface in contact and the speed of the motion. Modern friction theory views friction at the molecular level because friction is thought to be caused by molecular displacements.

When two surfaces contact each other, *adhesion* (attraction) forces arise between their respective molecules. A certain force parallel to the surfaces is needed to overcome the forces of adhesion and thus cause motion. The force is also required as the surfaces move relative to each other, as motion continually brings new adhesion points into contact.

According to these assumptions, friction should be proportional to the surface areas in contact. This disagrees with classical friction theory, which maintains that friction is indepen-

dent of contact area. The disparity can be explained, however. Ordinary and seemingly flat surfaces, when magnified at the molecular level, are seen as irregular as the surface of the moon. So contacts between surfaces involve only portions of their area.

If a solid object slides on a hard surface, contact is limited to a few points. Between these points, air or other materials separate the object and the underlying surface. The total area of the contact points is so small that it really does not depend on the area of the surfaces involved. The total contact area depends more directly on the relative hardness of the two contacting materials and on the weight of the sliding object.

The number of contact points increases with increasing weight. The total area of the contact points determines the magnitude of the friction. Friction then increases with and is proportional to weight over a relatively large range of weights, which agrees with older friction theory.

In air, the surfaces of solids are often covered by thin absorbing films of gas or liquid. These films separate objects from each other and influence friction through reduction of direct molecular contact, which therefore eases motion. As long as these films remain bound to the objects and are not freely detached, it's reasonable to assume that friction depends on the total area of points in contact.

Lubricants have long been known to reduce friction. But earlier explanations for this, involving the lubricant filling voids in the sliding surfaces, were incomplete.

Lubrication was more thoroughly explained by the "hydrodynamic ball-bearing theory," which contended that the friction between two lubricated machine parts was related to the internal friction, or viscosity, of the lubricant. This theory has been confirmed by experiments. The problems associated with pure liquid friction, which occurs when liquid layers completely separate mutually sliding surfaces, seem in principle to have been explained.

If an object moves on a liquid film on a flat surface, the liquid will be pressed to the side and, save for the absorption film, the object will come in contact with the underlying surface. So there is no liquid lubrication. Actually, liquid lubrication can occur only if the liquid pressed to the side is continually replaced.

In machines this type of lubrication is achieved by supplying lubricating liquid, usually through an oil hole. Liquid movement causes separation of the moving parts. Replacement of lubricating liquid pressed to the side can also occur through the sliding object being at an angle to the underlying surface, such as a sailboat sliding through water.

Friction on snow and ice resembles these basic forms of friction. But it is more complex because it is neither pure dry friction nor pure liquid friction.

Pure liquid friction is the easiest to understand. Transitional forms between pure liquid friction and pure dry friction, which are called "partly dry" or "mixed" friction, have yet to be explained completely.

Partly dry friction occurs when the liquid cannot support the force of the weight applied. Part of the force is then absorbed through elastic deformation of the irregularities in the contacting surfaces. Properties and characteristics depend on how the force between the surfaces is applied. If liquid supports most of the force, friction will be closest to liquid friction; if not, it will be closer to dry friction.

This introductory material is intended to serve as a basis for the following considerations of friction between skis and snow. Why is it easier to glide on snow and ice, for instance, than on asphalt or gravel? Through the years many theories have been advanced to explain the unique friction characteristics of snow. There are too many theories to explain fully here, but a short overview of the more important theories follows.

In the mid-19th century it was thought that ice particles, even at subfreezing temperatures, were surrounded by an extremely thin liquid-like film which acted as a lubricant. This old theory has recently been confirmed:

research has shown that liquid surface layers do exist.

Lubrication by water produced by melting due to pressure is another popular theory. However, the pressure under skis is so small that pressure-melting can be an important factor only at temperatures just below freezing, from -2° C to 0° C (28° to 32° F).

A friction-melting theory was developed by Bowden and Hughes in 1939 and is still one of the most quoted theories to explain ski glide. In short, the theory states that the friction of the skis gliding on the snow produces heat which then warms the snow to produce a thin liquid film on which the ski glides. However, simple computations show that the heat produced by ski glide is insufficient. Therefore the theory cannot fully explain ski glide, and it fails particularly for lower ski speeds. Other explanations are needed.

Recently Japanese scientists have concluded that the mechanical properties of ice (high hardness, low shear strength) are important. This makes ice unique among the more common solids such as stone, metal, and wood. Modern theories of dry friction, taking into account the properties of ice, partly explain low glide friction especially at lower glide speeds. The factors affecting glide, or the *kinematic friction coefficient*, are

- normal force, that is, skier weight,
- glide area, that is, ski contact area,
- glide speed,
- snow and air temperature conditions,
- shape, size, and degree of ski base irregularities (base preparation),

- ski base chemical composition and molecular structure,
- ski base mechanical and thermal properties,
- ski wax properties (application method, hardness, viscosity, melting point, chemical purity),
- ice and snow properties (crystal shape and size, crystal orientation, density, water content, pollution, hardness, plowing resistance, etc.).

For the sake of explanation, let's consider glide from the view of a skier gliding at constant speed under constant external conditions (snow, temperature, skis, etc.). At constant speed, all energy of motion is expended in overcoming various forms of friction:

- air resistance,
- plowing resistance (moving and compacting snow particles in making ski tracks),
- dry friction,
- wet friction.

From wind-tunnel measurements we know that air is the largest resistance to motion at high skiing speeds such as in ski jumping and downhill ski racing. This is why factors such as crouch positions and low-drag clothing are important in these events.

Plowing resistance can be considerable in loose snow or poor tracks. But racers are seldom in situations of having to push snow to the side. On Alpine courses and in cross-country tracks, plowing resistance is not important as long as the snow is not sopping wet. Dry and wet friction, then, are the forms important in skiing.

Dry friction can be large at low glide speeds. Considering

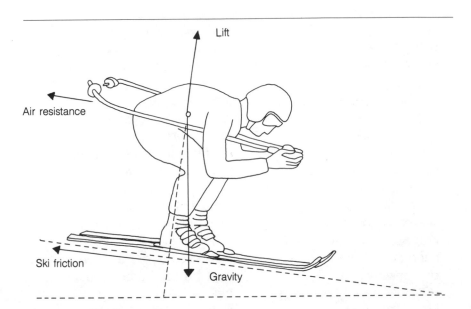

Arrows show forces acting on downhill skier.

that snow and plastic ski bases are both viscoelastic materials, theory agrees fairly well with practice. At higher skiing speeds, however, wet friction is also a factor. For viscoelastic materials, total contact area depends not only on weight but also on the shape of the surfaces and the duration of contact.

When calculating liquid friction, we must consider the five known possible sources of water/liquid in the ski-snow transition:

- Thin, liquid-like films have been observed on ice crystals. They have been computed to be 150 Å (Å for angstrom unit, 1/10,000,000 of a millimeter) at 0⁰ C (32⁰ F). Film thickness decreases to 10 Å as temperature falls to − 6⁰/ − 10⁰ (43⁰/50⁰ F). Snow crystals always contain some impurities, and the degree of impurity apparently affects film thickness. Research is now being conducted in Norway to determine the effect of pollutants on snow friction.

- Pressure melting, which is known to occur between 0⁰ and -2⁰ C (32⁰ to 28⁰ F);
- Friction melting, which may be important at high speeds but most likely is overvalued;
- Water contacting ice from thawing and freezing processes (rain and melt water);
- Precipitation in the form of supercooled water drops and condensed water vapor.

In the total picture of wet friction, the ultrathin 10-150 Å liquid-like film coating provides inadequate lubrication for the low friction on ice and snow. The amount of water supplied by friction melting is also so small that by itself it cannot cause glide.

This means that the various processes of dry and wet friction must be combined. Thus, one thing is certain: *The good glide of skis on ice and snow is not due to just one physical process. It is due to several processes acting together.* The contributions of each can vary, depending on how close the temperature is to freezing.

Some experiments indicate that dry friction is the most important type. This means that gliding skis come in direct contact with the ice crystals in the underlying snow and that ski motion deforms and breaks the crystals.

Static friction—grip of the cross-country skiing kick

Thus far we've discussed gliding friction. Cross-country skiing on flat terrain and up hills also depends on ski grip for the kick that provides forward power. Good grip depends on high static friction; slippery skis have too little static friction. The scientific reasons for static friction are better understood than the reasons for gliding friction.

A flat, weighted ski seems to make contact with the underlying snow throughout the length of its base. However, actual ski-base-to-snow contact is far less; when seen microscopically, only a few points are found to be in direct contact. High static friction occurs at these points when a ski glide stops for a brief 1/10 to 2/10 of a second just before a kick.

Snow particles can dig into the waxed base surface if it suits particle penetration ability. If a ski slips, it is because the wax is too hard. If the wax is too soft, the snow particles penetrate it so deeply that they are not brushed off by the following ski glide, thus allowing the ski to collect snow and to ice up. When the snow contains free water, snow particle penetration ability is low. Soft waxes are then needed to prevent skis from slipping.

Ski grip also depends on track quality. For instance, in klister conditions, in-track and out-of-track skiing are considerably different. Grip is least on ice, but it increases as snow particle size decreases. So, relatively soft waxes—"ice klisters"—are used for grip in cold, icy conditions, whereas hard waxes are used for fresh snow at the same temperature.

3 Ski Base Materials

Polyethylene is now the best and most used ski base material. There are many different qualities of polyethylene, differing in durability, waxability, and glide properties. Racing skis have sintered polyethylene bases, which have good wax retention and can glide well.

Sintering involves agglomerating polyethylene par-

Cross-section of a high molecular polyethylene base, magnified 100 times.

ticles together under high pressure, about 10 MPa (1450 psi), and high temperature, about 200⁰ C (390⁰ F). Polyethylene is not a homogeneous material. It consists of small wafer-like crystals surrounded by less structured material. These two parts are called *crystalline* and *amorphous*.

When polyethylene is heated, some of its crystals start to melt before the material itself melts at 135⁰ C (275⁰ F).

When wax is ironed into a ski base, as molten wax it

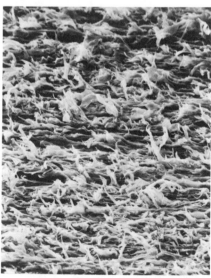

Factory-new ski base, not ground, magnified 100 times.

penetrates the spaces between the polyethylene crystals and mixes with the amorphous material. The extent of wax absorption depends on the volume of amorphous material. This means that the lower the density of the polyethylene, the more wax it can retain.

Temperature has proven to be important for wax penetration. About 100^0 to 110^0 C (212^0 to 230^0 F) is ideal, but higher temperature can easily damage a ski base. Wax retention also depends on time: Doubling the time the wax is on the base as a molten liquid can increase wax retention by 40%. At skiing temperatures of 0^0 C (32^0 F) and lower, the wax melted into the base *sweats* out of the base. However, compared to the speed of melting in, sweating out is slow, proceeding about 1/1000 as fast.

Ski base material can be degraded, or ''oxidized.''

Ultraviolet solar radiation together with oxygen and nitrogen in the air cause breakdown in the outermost layers of polyethylene. Therefore, bases should be protected with a layer of wax whenever skis are transported or stored. The protective wax is scraped off before the skis are used.

4 Ski Base Preparation and General Waxing Methods

Good glide is the goal of base preparation and waxing. The characteristics of the skiing surface—snow—vary considerably in hardness, particle size, density, and water content. So the aim of all methods used is to alter ski base characteristics accordingly. In short, base preparation amounts to altering sintered racing ski bases to suit various types of snow.

Test skiing and laboratory experiments have shown that smoothly polished ski bases do not glide as well as base surfaces that are slightly roughened with many small longitudinal grooves. This is why Alpine ski racers, and more recently cross-country ski racers, roughen or "structure" racing ski bases.

Surface roughness depends on snow temperature and wetness. The wetter the snow, the rougher the bases. The colder and newer the snow, the smoother the bases. Different base roughnesses are produced by sanding with different grit number sandpapers or by special rilling tools.

Silicon carbide sandpaper must be used, *not* the ordinary sandpaper as used for sanding wood. Sanding bases with different silicon carbide grit number papers produces a *macrostructure* that can be seen by the naked eye or with a magnifying glass. Sanding also produces a *microstructure* visible only under a microscope. Both the macrostructure and microstructure roughness should promote ski glide.

After sanding, bases should be polished with abrasive nylon pads such as Fiber-tex. This polishes the microstructure slightly while leaving the macrostructure unaffected. In addition to abrasives, brushes with different types of bristle are also used, most frequently after waxes have been applied and scraped down. Brushing removes wax in the depressions of the longitudinal grooved structure. Base preparation and waxing for glide overlap, then, and are discussed together (see page 42).

The procedure for preparing new skis differs from that for routine preparation of skis for different snow conditions, so the procedures will be described separately here.

New skis

Ski manufacturers use a variety of base grinding and final factory base treatment methods. Some of the preparation work may already have been done for you when the skis were prepared at the factory. In the factory, ski bases are usually sanded by machine, but the machine vibration may produce uneven ski bases. Furthermore, bases always collect some dust and dirt during transportation and storage, so some base preparation is always necessary.

The following procedure is recommended for Alpine and cross-country ski bases. Initially sand new ski bases with grit no. 100 paper, working with even strokes from tip to tail. When the

bases seem even and flat, stop sanding and remove all sanding dust. Next, sand with finer paper, grit no. 180, and again finish by removing all sanding dust.

Next, buff each ski base with a nylon fiber pad (Fiber-tex) for 5 to 10 minutes to remove the tiny rough hairs and fibers left by sanding. Work is sometimes eased by alternating buffing with brushing with a soft bronze or brass brush. Brushing lifts hairs that get pressed into the base during sanding, making them easier to remove. The same procedure can be used later if the bases are scratched in use.

Finally, treat the bases with Universal Glider or Violet Glider wax. First melt the wax onto the base, then iron it out, moving the iron back and forth so the wax is molten on the base.

transported or stored for a long time. Use the same procedure, but let the wax harden and don't scrape the bases until you use the skis. The wax protects the bases against oxidation and abrasion in transportation and storage.

In preparing new skis just before they are to be used in a race, use waxes similar to those to be used for the day's snow conditions. Don't glide wax the midzones of cross-country ski bases, but do apply a thin layer of cross-country grip wax, as it also protects the bases against oxidation.

Preparation and glide waxing for the day's conditions

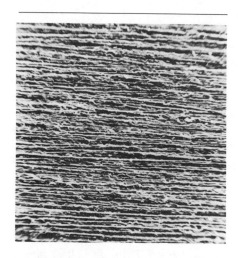

Ski base structured with grit no. 180 silicon carbide paper, followed by buffing with Fibertex, magnified 100 times.

Remove surplus surface wax while it is still molten, using a plastic scraper. This is the final cleaning process for removing sanding particles that were not removed in the preceding steps.

Add another layer of Glider wax on skis that are to be

Remove any transportation/storage wax. Decide what base structure matches the day's conditions. If it is the same as the structure put on the new ski bases, all that is required is to brush the bases with a bronze/brass brush and buff them with an abrasive nylon pad.

Select the glide wax for the day's conditions, melt it onto the bases, and warm it in with an iron or waxing iron. For a really

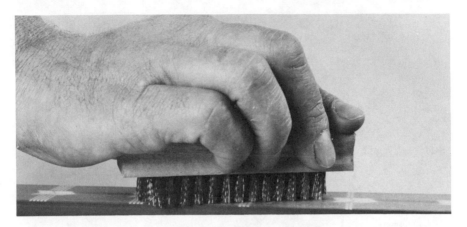

Brushing with a bronze/brass brush removes sanding dust and raises hairs pressed down in sanding.

First, heat the waxing iron.

Press the glide wax against the warmed iron to drip drops on both sides of the tracking groove.

Smooth the wax out with a warmed iron.

Use a plastic scraper to remove excess hardened wax from cooled skis.

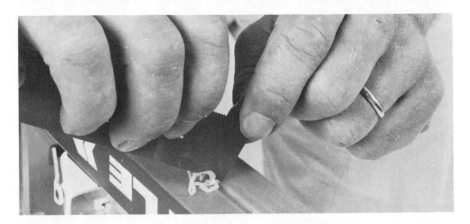

Don't forget to remove wax from the tracking groove; use a klister paddle.

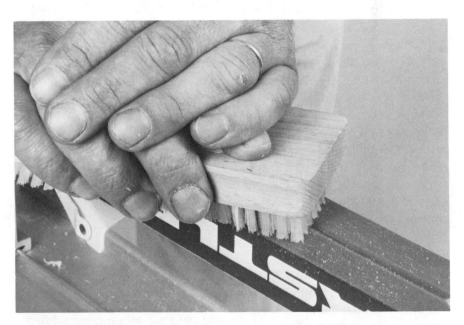

Finish glide waxing by brushing with a plastic brush to remove remaining wax from base structure.

thorough waxing, scrape off surplus wax while it is still warm and molten. This further adjusts the bases to the wax used. Then warm in a new layer of wax if necessary.

In any case, the final wax layer should cool and harden completely for about 30 minutes. Carefully scrape away surplus hardened wax with a plastic scraper. Metal scrapers are not recommended for this job because they can easily scar the base material. Don't forget to scrape wax out of the tracking groove and off the edges.

Next, brush the bases with a short, stiff nylon brush to remove smaller wax particles that scraping didn't remove from the base structure. Brush them a few more times, and now the skis are ready to use. Regardless of snow conditions or temperature, the bases should not be smoothed or polished after the final brushing.

Various snow conditions

Air temperature 0° C (32° F) and warmer

Old, heavy corn snow—klister conditions—call for removing all old wax and sanding the bases with grit no. 150 paper. Buff bases with a nylon pad and then brush with a bronze/brass brush. Finally, buff again with a nylon pad. Melt Red Glider wax on the tip and tail zones of the base and let it harden. Scrape with a plastic scraper and finish with a plastic brush.

Air temperature 0° to −7° C (32° to 19° F)

Start with clean skis and initially sand with grit no. 150 paper. Then sand tip and tail glide the zones with grit no. 180 paper, followed by alternate nylon pad buffing and bronze/brass brushing. Melt Violet Glider wax on, let it harden, scrape it down, and brush it with a plastic brush. Then scrape once more to remove all surplus wax. Finally, brush with a plastic brush.

Temperature −12° to −7° C (10° to 19° F)

Start with clean skis and lightly sand the midzones with grit no.

Use silicon carbide paper and a sanding block for structuring bases.

Buff with an abrasive nylon pad.

Rub hard wax on in short strokes on base.

Temperature under −20° C (−4° F)

Use the above procedure, except use grit no. 320 instead of no. 220 paper.

Grip zone waxing

150 paper. Sand the glide zones first with grit no. 180 paper, followed by grit no. 220 paper. Buff the entire base with a nylon pad, warm in Blue Glider wax, let it harden, and scrape it down. Finish with alternate plastic pad buffing and nylon brush brushing.

Temperature −20° to −12° C (−4° to 10° F)

Start with clean skis and first scrape the bases with a sharp plastic scraper. Then sand the glide zones with grit no. 220 paper and grip zones with no. 150 paper. Finish by buffing with a nylon pad. Warm in Green Glider wax, let it harden, and scrape it down. It's best to let prepared skis stand overnight. In the morning, scrape the bases once again and brush thoroughly with a nylon brush.

Sanding with grit no. 150 paper produces a good surface, and finishing with a nylon pad removes any dust and hairs from sanding. The procedure is the same as for the glide zones. Apply the wax of the day or, if necessary, an Orange Base Binder, in a thin, even layer. Iron the layer in to make it more durable, let the wax cool to room temperature, then smooth it out and polish it with a cork. Normally one or two more layers of wax are applied, preferably in cooler surroundings with corking between each layer.

Klister should also be warmed into the base. A torch flame is better than a waxing iron. Keep the flame moving, lest it play too long on one part of the base and overheat and damage the surface. When the first layer of klister has cooled, one or more additional layers may be applied without using heat. Smooth these layers out with a cork.

Use a synthetic cork to smooth wax.

Klister can be applied in a "herringbone" pattern.

Klister may also be applied in strips on either side of the tracking groove.

Spread klister smooth using the paddle packed with each tube.

Klister is quickly and easily smoothed with a waxing cork. Use separate corks for hard wax and for klister.

5 Waxes and Wax Types

As the term implies, the most basic constituent of ski wax is wax. In the early days of ski wax production, from 1900 to 1940, beeswax was the most commonly used type. Other animal and vegetable waxes were also used, but for several reasons they are less suitable for ski wax than mineral waxes are.

Chemically, mineral waxes are saturated hydrocarbons and have melting points from 40° to 100° C (104° to 212° F). Of the mineral waxes, *petroleum waxes* are now the major raw materials used in ski waxes. They are obtained from the refining of crude oils, some of which are more suitable than others for refining to petroleum waxes. For instance, crude oil from the offshore oil fields in the North Sea was originally refined to obtain other petroleum products but was subsequently used in wax production.

There are two types of petroleum waxes: paraffin and microcrystalline. Petroleum waxes are hydrocarbons whose constituent molecules have about 18 to 70 carbon atoms and twice as many hydrogen atoms.

As the name indicates, *microcrystalline* waxes are composed of minute crystals, far smaller than those of paraffin waxes. Paraffin wax molecules are mostly long chains, while microcrystalline wax molecules are mostly ring forms. Paraffin waxes are generally harder and more brittle than microcrystalline waxes, which tend to be softer and more flexible. Usually the melting points of paraffin waxes are the lower of the two. *Resins* are another important raw material and are used mostly in klisters and in klisterwax mixtures.

Ski waxes are divided into four convenient categories:

* cross-country hard waxes,
* Alpine and cross-country glide waxes,
* cross-country klisters,
* cross-country base binders.

Cross-country hard waxes

The pure waxes are too hard to both grip and glide, so oils are used to attain suitable consistency. Rubber additives are often used for the durability required of cross-country waxes.

Alpine and cross-country glide waxes

Waxes for Alpine skiing, ski jumping, and glide waxing of cross-country skis are compounded to glide as well as possible. They are based mostly on pure waxes. Quality must be high, so fully refined products that contain very little oil or other impurities are used. In fact, the stringent quality requirements are the same as those for waxes used in food packaging and in pharmaceuticals.

Just as the hardness of cross-country waxes vary to suit different snows, glide waxes are made in different hardnesses. Glide waxes for cold new snow are the hardest, while glide waxes for old, wet corn snow are the softest. Different hardnesses are obtained by using waxes with differing melting points and hardnesses, and by exploiting the differences in hardness between paraffin waxes and microcrystalline waxes.

Cross-country klisters

The earliest klisters contained natural pine tar. Although traditionalists may miss the aroma of pine tar, pine tars vary considerably in quality and otherwise cannot compete with modern synthetic resins. Modern klisters are very stable, odorless, and almost colorless. As for waxes, they are softened with oils since their chief constituents are otherwise too hard and brittle at low temperatures.

Rubber compounds are used to make klisters wear-resistant. Ice klister, for the most abrasive conditions, contains the most rubber. Wet snow klisters, for less abrasive conditions, contain the most oil.

Cross-country base binders

Cross-country base binder waxes differ from other cross-country waxes both in composition and purpose. The two types of Orange Base Binder provide a base for other hard waxes and are used when the snow is old and course. Their purpose is to improve final wax durability and reduce wearing.

Base binders contain both resin and rubber components, which is why they provide a tough surface to snow. But because they also slow the glide slightly, they should be completely covered with the wax of the day. Green klister may be used as a base binder to improve durability and wear resistance of other types of klister.

Waxes match skier needs

There are now more types of wax than ever before. Just 25 years ago there were three hard waxes and two klisters. Since then, new waxes of differing composition and hardness have been developed. At the same time, racing has advanced considerably and racers have continuously pushed the limits of ski grip and glide. The greater number of waxes now available has made waxing neither easier nor more complex, but rather has given racers greater choice in waxes to meet individual needs.

In reading the directions on a wax tin or tube, remember that there is an infinite variety of snow types and conditions but only a limited number of waxes to match those conditions. This means that the fewer waxes there are in a series, the greater range each type must be capable of.

The variability of snow and the nature of wax also makes it impossible to define wax ranges exactly. There is always some overlap between adjacent waxes in a series, though each will have its own ideal range. The ideal range of a wax is the range of snow conditions for which its grip and glide are optimum. The further away from the ideal range, the greater the chance of slippery or sticky skis.

Usually air temperatures are used to define the ideal ranges for waxes stated on the tins and tubes, but for racers temperature alone isn't an adequate guide to wax selection. Humidity is also important. At 90% or more relative humidity, waxes must be selected 2º to 3º C (4º to 5º F) "warmer" than indicated by the directions on the container. Conversely, for extremely dry conditions wax may be selected

"colder." A rule of thumb in selection is that the temperature range indicated on the container is correct for a relative humidity of 60% to 70%. Corrections for other humidity conditions are most important for fresh and falling snow.

Hard waxes

Let's look at hard waxes, beginning with the hardest.

Polar

The maker designation *Alaska* is also used for this wax, which is suitable for extreme cold. It is used for new snow at temperatures of -12º C (10º F) and below, and for older snow at -15º C (5º F) and below. The composition and hardness of

Polar also make it suitable for use on tip and tail glide zones, particularly on courses requiring good grip. The colder the conditions, the less important it is to have pure glide wax on the tip and tail glide zones.

Green Special

This wax has an ideal range of -9° to -12° C (16° to 10° F) on new snow and -11° to -15° C (12° to 5° F) on more corned snow.

Green

Unless they ski in extremely cold conditions, most recreational skiers never need a harder wax than Green. Its ideal range is -8° to -10° C (18° to 14° F) on new snow and about -9° to -12° C (16° to 10° F) on older snow.

Green Extra

This is a soft version of Green and is used frequently by racers. It is used on new snow between -6° and -9° C (21° and 16° F) and on older snow between -8° and -10° C (18° and 14° F).

Blue Special

This is the hard version of the Blue first used in the 1980 Winter Olympics in Lake Placid. Its hardness and consistency place it between Green Extra and Blue. Its ideal range is -5° to -7° C (23° to 19° F) on falling or fresh snow, and -6° to -8° C (21° to 18° F) on older snow.

Blue

This is the most popular of ski waxes, the standby for recreational skiers and racers alike. It covers the temperature range from -2° to -5° C (28° to 23° F) on new snow and -3° to -7° C

(27⁰ to 19⁰ F) on fine-grained snow.

Blue Extra

This wax, frequently used by racers, is softer than Blue and therefore has better grip. The ideal range on new snow is from around -2⁰ C up to near 0⁰ C (28⁰ to 32⁰ F). In this temperature range, consideration of humidity is important in selecting wax, especially if super-cooled rain falls on the snow; in that case a softer wax than indicated by temperature is needed. In humid climates and during showers, Blue Extra is used down to -5⁰ to -6⁰ C (23⁰ to 21⁰ F). Racers who wax short kickers often use Blue Extra for conditions under which recreational skiers would best wax their entire ski bases with Blue.

Violet Special

This wax falls between Blue Extra and Violet in hardness and was first used at the 1982 FIS World Ski Championships in Oslo. Violet Special is a typical freezing-point wax, but its ideal range is just under freezing. When the temperature is just below freezing and the humidity is high, or when there's fog in the air, Blue Extra sometimes grips poorly. For these conditions Violet Special is the better wax.

Violet

This wax is used for transition conditions from dry to wet snow in mild weather with the temperature around 0⁰ C (32⁰ F). Violet is often used along with adjacent waxes in the spectrum. For instance, it is used to adjust Blue Extra or Violet Special for better grip, and it is used as a base layer for Red Special. For these conditions, it is best to start with a harder wax and gradually work in softer waxes until grip is satisfactory.

Wax layer thickness is also important. Waxing too thick may result in icing and snow buildup on skis. Note that at temperatures around the freezing point, wax must be skied in for a few hundred yards before it works right. Normally if the right wax is chosen and applied properly, skis will initially be slippery but will rapidly stabilize to good grip and glide.

Red Special

This wax has an ideal range just above freezing for falling or newly fallen snow. These are usually difficult waxing conditions, as small temperature variations can alternately cause icing and slipping. Because of its built-in flexibility, Red Special is the most frequently used wax for such difficult conditions. But be careful not to apply it too thick. Start with a thin layer; if it doesn't grip, maybe a thin additional layer of a softer wax will work.

Red

This is also an important wax that belongs in everyone's wax kit. It is used on particularly moist, sticky snow at air temperatures a few degrees above freezing, and also when snow is new or fine-grained, having been through several melt-freeze cycles. Recreational skiers often use Red wax when racers pick a stickier Yellow Klisterwax, which can be difficult to apply evenly.

Red Extra

This is a relatively new variety of basic Red, with a consistency similar to a klisterwax. Red Extra is frequently used on snows where water content is increasing, such as on tracks in new snow exposed to strong sunshine. The air temperature may be around 5⁰ C (41⁰ F), but snow consistency is more important than temperature in selecting wax. In other words, how long is has been warm is more important than how warm it is at the moment.

Klisterwax

Yellow Klisterwax is used on moist and sticky new snow, but be careful: don't apply it too thick! Klisterwax is definitely called for when tracks turn to glazed, slithering rails. If conditions are mushy, then it's already time for klister. But skiing out of tracks and into new snow will often ice klisterwax. Klisterwax is so soft and sticky that it can be "punched" onto bases rather than rubbed on like the other hard waxes.

Orange Base Binder wax

There are two varieties of Orange Base Binder: soft and hard. The soft variety is identified by a blue belt on the tin and has an ideal range from 0⁰ to -5⁰ C (32⁰ to 23⁰ F). The hard variety is identified by a green belt on the tin and has an ideal range from -5⁰ C down to about -18⁰ C (23⁰ to 0⁰ F). Both types should be carefully ironed to a thin layer on clean ski bases. After the binder has cooled and hardened, apply a couple layers of the day's wax.

Other waxes

We have discussed waxes in order of decreasing hardness and have included waxes that are suitable for most snow conditions.

tain snow conditions exactly, even though they are intended for average recreational use on all snows.

Klisters

Two wax systems are also available. They are intended for recreational skiers who are not very interested in waxing or the performance of well waxed skis. Two-wax systems consist of one wax for below freezing and one wax for above freezing conditions. The harder, Gold wax for cold conditions has an ideal range between Blue and Blue Extra, but is slightly more durable. The softer wax for warmer conditions contains metal particles which give it a silver color and make it less sticky than Red or Red Extra. It is made to cover the entire range of wet snows. The wetter the snow, the thicker the wax layer.

Experienced skiers and racers occasionally use these waxes. As long as they are of the same high quality as other waxes, it is obvious that they may suit cer-

In general, klister snow conditions can be defined as different from hard wax snow conditions. But there are also intermediate conditions in which both klisters and hard waxes work, either by themselves or in combination with each other.

- When the snow is so wet that the softest hard waxes, Red Extra and Klisterwax, don't grip well, it's a klister condition.
- When snow has been corned by one or more melting-freezing cycles, it's a klister condition.

Green Klister

This is the hardest, toughest klister and is recommended as a binder for other klisters for longer distance skiing in abrasive snows. Green Klister may also be used by itself, in icy tracks at temperatures of -10⁰ C (14⁰ F) or colder. Green Klister is so tough that it doesn't crack and flake off as many other types of klister do.

Blue Klister

This is the most widely used ice klister, both for recreational skiing and racing. It is used in icy tracks and on old, heavy corn snow, especially snow that is altered by melting and freezing in the upper layers. Air temperatures can range from -4° to -10° C (25° to 14° F). Like Green Klister, Blue Klister is a good base binder for Violet, Silver, and Red klisters.

Violet Special Klister

This is a new klister with an ideal range below freezing; it is recommended for temperatures from 0° to -4° C (32° to 25° F).

Violet Klister

This klister spans the critical range just above and below freezing. It is one of the most important waxes and belongs in everyone's wax kit. Violet Klister suits changing conditions, from icy to moist, rough snow. It works in these variable conditions because the properties of heavy corn snow particles in contact with air don't change as air temperature changes while hovering around freezing.

Red Special Klister

The consistency of this klister places it between Violet Klister and Red Klister. Its ideal temperature range is just above freezing. It is typically used when snow, once hard and icy, is now melting and becoming wet with free water but is not yet mushy or thoroughly wet. Red Special is also used over Violet for better grip in rising temperatures.

Red Klister

This is the standby wet-snow klister. It is suitable for the thoroughly wet, heavy corn snows of late winter, early spring, or midwinter thaws. Red Klister is the softest of all ski waxes, so it is used on snows where the snow and ice particles penetrate wax poorly.

We have discussed klisters in order of decreasing hardness, from Green to Red. There are also four other types of klisters that cannot be classified directly on the scale of hardness because each has unique properties.

Silver Special Klister

This klister has an ideal temperature range from 0° to 3° C (32° to 37° F) but is used when snow particle size and water content are more important considerations than air temperature. It contains fine aluminum particles which give it its silver color and its name. The aluminum particles increase klister hardness and make it less sticky, thus rendering it suitable even for finer, dryer sections of track.

Silver Klister

This is basically a wet-snow klister, softer than Silver Special and containing fewer aluminum particles. The aluminum particles make it less sticky than Red Klister. Silver Klister is basically intended for dirty and/or polluted snows, and therefore it is often mixed with Red Klister, especially in late winter when dirty snows usually cause the greatest waxing problems.

Yellow Klister

This klister has a small but vital range. Consider a situation with falling snow and rising temperature, with the snow gradually changing to rain and mist. Tracks glaze rapidly, apparently producing klisterwax conditions. But air humidity and water content are so high that hard waxes grip poorly. These are the conditions for Yellow Klister, which is less sticky and harder than Red Klister. Yellow Klister should be applied *thin*. However, it should *not* be used on snows that have undergone melting and refreezing and are melting anew. Those conditions call for Red Klister. Yellow Klister is a *new snow klister*.

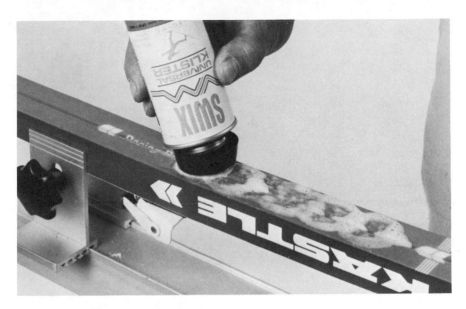

Aerosol klisters are easily and rapidly applied.

Universal Klister

Designing a wax as "universal" may be a bit pretentious, even though the term is scientifically more correct for klisters than for hard waxes. Universal Klister resembles Violet Klister, which might also be termed "universal" because it is suitable for snow conditions both above and below freezing. Yet it differs from Violet Klister in that its ideal range is suitable for snow that is more wet.

Now that you are aware of the various types of wax and how they are used, you should know that some klisters are also available in aerosol cans for speed and ease of application. Aerosol klisters contain solvents and propellant gas but otherwise are identical to tube klisters. However, the solvents must be allowed to evaporate before the skis are put on snow. Aerosol klisters are intended for skiers who wish to avoid working with ordinary klister or who prefer the neater, cleaner application that aerosols afford.

6 Removing Wax

There are two ways to remove wax and clean skis:

- Heating the wax with a torch and wiping the molten wax off the ski with a rag or a cloth;
- Dissolving the wax with a wax solvent and wiping the ski clean with cleaning tissue or a rag or cloth.

Regardless of which method you use, it's always best to start by removing as much wax as possible with a scraper. The less there is to remove, the easier the skis are to clean. The first method is generally *not* recommended, as torch heat may be so high that it can damage the ski base. In addition, wax on the base and any contaminants it may have picked up from dirty snow can be warmed into the base.

Dissolving with a solvent is the recommended method. Special wax-removing solvents are available, both as liquids and as aerosol sprays. (At this writing, strict restrictions on aerosols limit their availability in the USA.) When the wax on the ski is soaked with solvent, use a plastic scraper to remove as much dissolved wax as possible.

Then remove the rest with cleaning tissue such as Fiberlene. Finally, wipe the skis clean and dry with a clean dry cloth.

Many industrial or commercial solvents remove ski wax more effectively than do special wax removers offered by ski wax makers. However, these solvents all have one or more of the following drawbacks:

- They may be highly toxic.
- They are highly flammable and therefore cannot be used where waxing torches are used.
- They may produce allergic reactions.
- They may be hazardous to breathing in poorly ventilated rooms.

If solvents and wiping don't seem to clean skis completely, try light sanding as described on page 42. Molten wax can also be used as a cleaner, but cross-country waxes should not be used for cleaning bases.

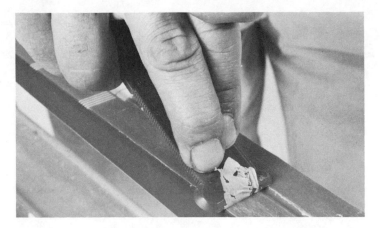

Start cleaning by scraping.

Special wax-removing solvents are recommended for cleaning skis.

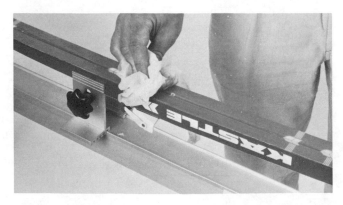

Remove dissolved wax with Fiberlene or a rag.

7 Waxing for Racing

Often you hear that racers placed poorly or lost because they "missed the wax." How can that be? How can experienced racers, backed by teammates, coaches, and perhaps even by racer chasers, wax incorrectly? The explanation is simple. In racing, seconds and tenths of seconds count. When competition is keen, small deviations in waxing are decisive for result list placings.

In most cases, missing the wax means that the waxing job wasn't the best. A recreational skier might not have even noticed the difference and would have been pleased at least with ski glide.

What can you do to get good skis? Is there any way to avoid minor or major errors in wax selection? Before important races, you should have the opportunity to follow weather and snow conditions in the course terrain. Test wax, preferably the day before the race at the same time of day as the race. You can guard against changing weather conditions by trying two or three alternative waxings the day before the race so you have less to do on race day.

Glide wax should also be chosen and applied the day before the race, so on race day you need only select and apply grip wax. Team officials, coaches, nonracing teammates, or others can check conditions and waxing around the course in the hours before race time. On-course testing is especially useful if course topography varies considerably or if sun and cloud cover are changing.

But waxing shouldn't be overdone or made difficult. There's a limit to how much help and information you can use. If you have two-way radios or other communications, it is often helpful to station an observer at the highest (or coldest) point on the course to report conditions until the start. Don't spend so much time waxing that you do not have time to warm up before the start, however. Choose wax using reliable air temperature and snow temperature measurements and, if possible, relative humidity measurements.

Experience is unquestionably the best guide. Training is the time to experiment with waxes and learn all about them. Too many racers fall prey to prerace nerves and totally neglect the skills and judgment they have built up during their training. This is not the time to be careless. Racers must put their experience with waxing to its best use when preparing to race.

Balancing grip and glide wax

The perennial question seems to be how long to wax for grip and where to wax for glide. There's no fixed formula that holds for all racers because so many individual factors are involved. Kick power, arm strength, ski stiffness, snow conditions, and so forth determine the balance of grip and glide that is best for each racer.

There are two guideline rules:

- For hard wax on dry snow, the grip zone should be 50 to 80 cm (20 to 30 in.) long.
- For klisters, the grip zone should be 40 to 60 cm (16 to 24 in.) long.

Most racing skis have "waxing marks" on their bases. During training, check wax length in terms of these marks. Try waxing different lengths of grip wax on the two skis of a pair, and ski on the pair for a right-left comparison.

Hard wax or klister?

As a general rule, klister should be used on snow that

has melted and frozen at least once. However, modern machine course preparation and track setting has altered that general rule somewhat. The preparation machines pulverize the hard packed snow and leave fine snow particles in the tracks. While the off-course snow conditions may call for klister, hard wax may work best in the course tracks. The lower the temperature, the more likely that a combination of one of the Orange Base Binder waxes and a hard wax suiting the temperature will both grip and glide better than klister. This is because the hard, pulverized snow particles tend to penetrate deep into klister and stay there, forming a thin ice layer; the skis are both slow and slippery.

At temperatures near freezing, klister is again equal to or better than hard wax. However, for some transition conditions klister is best as a first layer, covered by Blue or Violet hard wax. In-track ski testing is the only way to find out what works best.

Harder wax on top of softer

The general rule for waxing is to start with harder waxes and perhaps apply softer waxes on top of them. But racing waxing often deviates from that rule. The chief reason for applying harder wax on top of softer wax is to protect the softer wax against undercooling and freezing.

A typical situation might be a race in which the snow at the start/finish is new and wet, calling for Red Special hard wax. Higher on the course there might be new snow, with temperatures reported one or two degrees colder. The softer Red Special needed in the start/finish area can be protected with a layer of Blue Extra. The grip at lower course elevations will still be acceptable, while the risk of icing at higher elevations will be reduced.

The first layer should be applied using ordinary waxing techniques. Then the skis should be allowed to cool before the harder wax is applied. Application is easiest if the wax is softened in a torch flame for an instant and then rubbed on with a cork while it is still warm and soft. Excessively hard rubbing should be avoided, as it blends the two waxes instead of preserving their individual characteristics.

The same techniques are used to cover klister with hard wax. First, klister is warmed into the base and the skis are cooled. Then the hard wax is warmed slightly and carefully rubbed out over the cooled klister.

Abrading

Abrading is a technique developed by American racers. It was first used internationally by Bill Koch in the 1982 Swedish Ski Games 30-km race. In principle, abrading involves working the grip zone of ski bases with rough abrading tools that raise many small polyethylene hairs up from the base. Each raised hair acts as a small sawtooth and will grip on the right snow conditions. The method has limits, of course, but its ideal range is exactly where conventional waxing most often is difficult, so it's very useful for racers.

The right snow conditions for this method involve falling or newly fallen wet or extremely moist snow. If the snow has turned to corn, abrading won't pro-

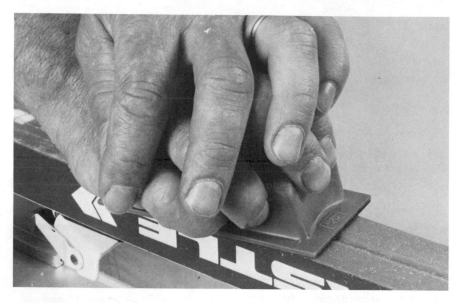

Use a rasp to abrade grip zone.

Silicone liquid protects the abraded zone.

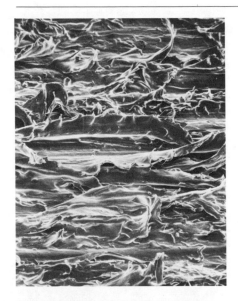

Electron microscope photo of an abraded base. The individual fibers act as sawteeth, giving grip for kick when snow conditions are right for this method.

80 silicon carbide paper, or preferably with a rasp. Then loose dust is brushed off with a bronze/brass brush. Finally the abraded region is coated with silicone liquid, such as Sarajevo Special, which prevents freezing and matting of the hairs. Warming the ski base slightly before the silicone liquid is applied aids its penetration.

Abraded skis must be scraped and sanded smooth before being waxed for other snow conditions. Repeated abrading will of course finally eat up the base. So it's an expensive way to wax if you have to buy skis.

vide adequate grip. The snow has to be wet enough for the method to work; it doesn't work on dry snow.

Abrading involves the grip zone only; tips and tails are glide waxed as usual. First the grip zone in the center of the ski is roughened with grit no. 60 or

References

Literature cited

Bowden, F.P., & Hughes, T.P. (1939). *The mechanism of sliding on ice and snow.* Proc. R. Soc., Series A., **172**, 280-298.

Magono, C., & Lee, C.W. (1966). *Meteorological classification of natural snow crystals.* J. Faculty Science, Hokkaido Univ., Sapporo, Japan, Series VII

(Geophysics), **2**(4), 321-335; available in reprint from Rocky Mountain Forest and Range Experimental Station, Fort Collins, CO.

Reference books

Much of the research in the snow sciences is devoted to avalanche safety and control. Therefore, most books on snow focus on avalanche problems. Three good reference books are:

Daffern, T. (1983). *Avalanche safety for skiers & climbers*, Alpenbooks, Seattle and Rocky Mountain Books, Calgary.

Gray, D.M., & Male, D.H. (Eds.) (1981). *Handbook of snow*. Pergamon Press, Toronto, New York, Oxford.

Perla, R.I., & Martinelli, M. (Eds.) (1976). *Avalanche handbook*. Agriculture Handbook 489, U.S. Dept. of Agriculture, Forest Service.